Liechtenstein

Everything You Need to Know

Copyright © 2024 by Noah Gil-Smith.

All rights reserved. No part of this book may be reproduced, distributed, or transmitted in any form or by any means, including photocopying, recording, or other electronic or mechanical methods, without the prior written permission of the publisher, except in the case of brief quotations embodied in critical reviews and certain other noncommercial uses permitted by copyright law. This book was created with the assistance of Artificial Intelligence. The content presented in this book is for entertainment purposes only. It should not be considered as a substitute for professional advice or comprehensive research. Readers are encouraged to independently verify any information and consult relevant experts for specific matters. The author and publisher disclaim any liability or responsibility for any loss, injury, or inconvenience caused or alleged to be caused directly or indirectly by the information presented in this book.

Introduction to Liechtenstein 6

The History of Liechtenstein: From Earliest Settlements to Modern Times 9

Princely Beginnings: The Rise of the Liechtenstein Dynasty 12

Liechtenstein's Unique Political Landscape: A Principality's Governance 14

Liechtenstein's Geography: Nestled in the Heart of Europe 16

Exploring Liechtenstein's Natural Beauty: Landscapes and Wildlife 18

Alpine Adventures: Outdoor Activities in Liechtenstein 20

Liechtenstein's Economic Success Story: From Agriculture to Finance 22

Vaduz: The Charming Capital City of Liechtenstein 25

Balzers: A Glimpse into Liechtenstein's Rural Charm 27

Schaan: Industrial Hub and Cultural Center 29

Triesen: A Historical Journey through Liechtenstein's Past 31

Mauren: Traditions and Modernity Intertwined 34

The Rich Cultural Tapestry of Liechtenstein: Arts and Festivals 36

Liechtenstein's Culinary Delights: A Fusion of Alpine and International Flavors 38

Winegrowing in Liechtenstein: A Tradition of Quality and Excellence 40

The Language of Liechtenstein: A Blend of German Dialects 43

Education in Liechtenstein: Nurturing Minds in a Principality 45

The Liechtensteinische Landesmuseum: Preserving the Nation's Heritage 47

Vaduz Castle: The Iconic Symbol of Liechtenstein 49

The Princely Collection: Art Treasures of Liechtenstein's Rulers 51

Gutenberg Castle: A Medieval Marvel in Liechtenstein 53

St. Florin Cathedral: Religious Heritage in Liechtenstein 55

The Kunstmuseum Liechtenstein: Contemporary Art in a Historical Setting 57

Skiing in Malbun: Winter Sports Paradise in Liechtenstein 59

The Walser Museum: Exploring Liechtenstein's Alpine Heritage 61

Liechtenstein's Banking Sector: A Pillar of Stability 63

The Liechtenstein Institute: Promoting Research and Dialogue 65

The Philately Museum: A Stamp Collector's Haven 67

Liechtenstein National Library: A Treasure Trove of Knowledge 69

The Liechtenstein Red Cross: Humanitarian Efforts in the Principality 71

Liechtenstein's Transportation Infrastructure: Connecting Communities 73

Sustainable Development in Liechtenstein: Balancing Progress and Preservation 75

Citizenship and Immigration in Liechtenstein: Rights and Responsibilities 77

Liechtenstein's Role in European Affairs: A Neutral Player's Perspective 80

Royal Residences: Palaces and Estates of Liechtenstein's Princely Family 83

Liechtenstein's Philharmonic Orchestra: A Cultural Jewel in the Alps 85

Religious Diversity in Liechtenstein: Coexistence and Harmony 87

Liechtenstein's Sporting Achievements: Small Nation, Big Successes 90

Philately and Numismatics: Liechtenstein's Contributions to the World of Collecting 93

Liechtenstein's Health Care System: Prioritizing Well-being for All 96

Family Life in Liechtenstein: Traditions and Values Passed Down Generations 99

Environmental Conservation in Liechtenstein: Preserving the Alpine Ecosystem 101

Future Prospects: Challenges and Opportunities for Liechtenstein 104

Epilogue 106

Introduction to Liechtenstein

Nestled in the heart of Europe, Liechtenstein stands as a testament to the charm and resilience of small nations. Despite its diminutive size, this tiny Alpine gem boasts a rich tapestry of history, culture, and natural beauty waiting to be discovered. Bordered by Switzerland to the west and south and Austria to the east and north, Liechtenstein occupies a mere 160 square kilometers, making it one of the smallest countries in the world. Yet, within its borders lies a wealth of treasures that captivate the imagination and inspire exploration.

With a population of approximately 38,000 inhabitants, Liechtenstein maintains a close-knit community that takes pride in its unique identity. The country is a constitutional monarchy, with a parliamentary democracy and a hereditary monarchy at its helm. At the pinnacle of its political structure sits the Prince of Liechtenstein, currently Prince Hans-Adam II, whose lineage traces back to the 17th century when the principality was established.

The history of Liechtenstein is intertwined with the rise and fall of empires, the struggles of feudal lords, and the aspirations of its people. Originally inhabited by Celts and later settled by the Romans, the territory of modern-day Liechtenstein witnessed successive waves of migration and conquest before eventually falling under the sway of the Holy Roman Empire. It was during this time that the Liechtenstein family, hailing from the Rhine Valley, rose to prominence, acquiring land and titles that would form the nucleus of the principality.

In 1719, Liechtenstein was officially recognized as a sovereign territory within the Holy Roman Empire, and over the centuries, it weathered wars, political upheavals, and economic challenges. However, it wasn't until the aftermath of World War II that Liechtenstein truly began to emerge as a modern state. With the decline of agriculture and the rise of financial services, Liechtenstein transitioned from a predominantly rural economy to a global player in banking and finance.

Today, Liechtenstein stands as a beacon of prosperity and stability, boasting one of the highest standards of living in the world. Its economy thrives on a mix of industries, including manufacturing, tourism, and finance, while its commitment to environmental sustainability sets an example for nations far beyond its borders. Visitors to Liechtenstein are greeted by a landscape of breathtaking beauty, with snow-capped mountains, lush valleys, and picturesque villages dotting the countryside.

But Liechtenstein is more than just its stunning scenery and economic prowess. It is a nation with a rich cultural heritage, celebrated through art, music, and festivals that reflect its Alpine traditions and global outlook. Its capital, Vaduz, is a vibrant hub of activity, home to museums, galleries, and architectural wonders that showcase the country's past and present.

As we embark on a journey to explore Liechtenstein, let us delve into the intricacies of its history, geography, culture, and society. From the majestic peaks of the Alps to the quaint villages nestled in the valleys, there is much to discover and appreciate in this small yet remarkable country. So, join me as we uncover the wonders of Liechtenstein and unravel the secrets of its enduring allure.

The History of Liechtenstein: From Earliest Settlements to Modern Times

The history of Liechtenstein is a captivating tale that unfolds across centuries, tracing the footsteps of ancient civilizations, medieval lords, and modern-day monarchs. Situated in the heart of Europe, this small principality has witnessed the ebb and flow of empires, the rise and fall of dynasties, and the evolution of society and culture.

The story of Liechtenstein begins thousands of years ago, with evidence of human habitation dating back to the Neolithic period. Inhabited by Celtic tribes and later settled by the Romans, the region that would become Liechtenstein was a crossroads of trade and migration, nestled between the mighty Rhine River and the towering peaks of the Alps.

With the collapse of the Roman Empire, the territory of Liechtenstein fell under the sway of various Germanic tribes, including the Alemanni and the Franks. By the early Middle Ages, the area was part of the lands governed by the Duchy of Swabia within the Holy Roman Empire, a patchwork of feudal territories and ecclesiastical states.

It was during this time that the Liechtenstein family, originally from the Rhine Valley in what is now Austria and Switzerland, began to rise to prominence. Acquiring land and titles through strategic alliances and feudal patronage, the

Liechtensteins established themselves as powerful lords in the region, eventually acquiring the lordship of Schellenberg in 1699 and the county of Vaduz in 1712.

In 1719, Emperor Charles VI of the Holy Roman Empire united the lordships of Schellenberg and Vaduz into a single principality and bestowed upon the Liechtenstein family the title of "prince," in honor of their loyalty and service to the empire. Thus, the Principality of Liechtenstein was born, named after the Liechtenstein family who would govern it for centuries to come.

Throughout the 18th and 19th centuries, Liechtenstein navigated the turbulent waters of European politics, maintaining its independence and neutrality amidst the upheavals of war and revolution. Despite its small size, Liechtenstein managed to carve out a niche for itself, relying on agriculture, trade, and diplomacy to sustain its economy and preserve its sovereignty.

The dawn of the 20th century brought new challenges and opportunities for Liechtenstein, as the world plunged into two devastating world wars. Despite its landlocked position and lack of natural resources, Liechtenstein managed to weather the storms of conflict, emerging from the chaos of war relatively unscathed.

In the post-war era, Liechtenstein embarked on a path of modernization and diversification, transforming its economy from agriculture to industry and finance. Leveraging its strategic location, favorable tax laws, and political stability, Liechtenstein became a global hub for banking and financial services, attracting businesses and investors from around the world.

Today, Liechtenstein stands as a testament to the resilience and adaptability of small nations in the face of adversity. With its prosperous economy, stable government, and commitment to sustainability, Liechtenstein continues to thrive in the 21st century, while remaining true to its rich heritage and traditions.

Princely Beginnings: The Rise of the Liechtenstein Dynasty

The rise of the Liechtenstein dynasty is a saga steeped in the annals of European history, spanning centuries of intrigue, ambition, and fortune. Originating from humble beginnings in the Rhine Valley, the Liechtenstein family's ascent to prominence began in the medieval era, when feudal lords wielded power and influence over the lands they governed.

The earliest recorded mention of the Liechtenstein family dates back to the 12th century, when they were known as the Lords of Liechtenstein, presiding over a small fiefdom in what is now Austria and Switzerland. Over time, the family expanded its holdings through marriage alliances, military conquests, and diplomatic maneuvering, solidifying its position as one of the region's most powerful noble houses.

It was during the 16th and 17th centuries that the Liechtenstein family's fortunes truly began to flourish, thanks in part to the patronage of the Holy Roman Emperors and their involvement in the affairs of state. Under the leadership of Karl I von Liechtenstein, the family amassed vast estates and acquired prestigious titles, including that of Imperial Prince.

In 1699, the Liechtenstein family acquired the lordship of Schellenberg, followed by the county of

Vaduz in 1712, laying the foundations for the future Principality of Liechtenstein. These acquisitions were instrumental in securing the family's status and influence within the Holy Roman Empire, paving the way for their elevation to princely rank.

In 1719, Emperor Charles VI of the Holy Roman Empire united the lordships of Schellenberg and Vaduz into a single principality and bestowed upon the Liechtenstein family the title of "prince," in recognition of their loyalty and service to the empire. This pivotal moment marked the official establishment of the Principality of Liechtenstein, named after the Liechtenstein family who would govern it for generations to come.

Throughout the centuries, the Liechtenstein dynasty continued to play a prominent role in European affairs, serving as advisors to emperors, generals in the military, and patrons of the arts. Their wealth and influence extended far beyond the borders of their tiny principality, shaping the course of history and leaving an indelible mark on the world stage.

Today, the Liechtenstein dynasty remains one of Europe's oldest and most esteemed noble houses, with Prince Hans-Adam II currently reigning as the head of the family and sovereign of the Principality of Liechtenstein. Despite the passage of time and the shifting tides of fortune, the legacy of the Liechtenstein dynasty endures, a testament to the enduring power of perseverance, ambition, and noble lineage.

Liechtenstein's Unique Political Landscape: A Principality's Governance

Liechtenstein's political landscape is as unique as the principality itself, blending elements of monarchy, democracy, and direct governance to create a system that is both traditional and modern. At its heart lies the princely house of Liechtenstein, headed by Prince Hans-Adam II, who serves as the sovereign ruler of the nation. The princely family's influence extends beyond mere figurehead status, playing an active role in shaping policy and governance.

Despite its royal lineage, Liechtenstein operates under a constitutional monarchy, with a parliamentary democracy that affords its citizens a voice in the affairs of state. The Constitution of Liechtenstein, adopted in 1921 and revised in 2003, outlines the framework of government and guarantees fundamental rights and freedoms to all citizens. The parliament, known as the Landtag, is composed of 25 members elected by universal suffrage for a term of four years.

The executive branch of government is led by the Prince, who appoints the head of government, known as the Prime Minister, as well as other members of the cabinet. While the Prince retains the power to veto legislation and dissolve the parliament, these powers are exercised in accordance with constitutional principles and the rule of law. In practice, the Prince's role is largely ceremonial, with day-to-day governance entrusted to elected representatives.

Liechtenstein's unique political system also includes elements of direct democracy, allowing citizens to participate directly in the legislative process through referendums and initiatives. This decentralized approach to governance empowers citizens to have a direct say in matters of public policy, ensuring that the government remains accountable and responsive to the will of the people.

In addition to its domestic governance, Liechtenstein also maintains a distinct position in international affairs, characterized by its commitment to neutrality and diplomacy. Despite its small size, Liechtenstein is a member of various international organizations, including the United Nations, the European Free Trade Association, and the Council of Europe. Its diplomatic corps works tirelessly to promote peace, human rights, and economic cooperation on the global stage.

Overall, Liechtenstein's political landscape reflects a delicate balance between tradition and modernity, monarchy and democracy, sovereignty and international engagement. As the principality continues to evolve and adapt to the challenges of the 21st century, its unique political system remains a testament to the resilience and ingenuity of its people.

Liechtenstein's Geography: Nestled in the Heart of Europe

Liechtenstein's geography is nothing short of picturesque, a landscape that seems straight out of a storybook nestled snugly in the heart of Europe. Situated between Switzerland to the west and south and Austria to the east and north, this tiny principality spans just 160 square kilometers, making it one of the smallest countries in the world. Despite its diminutive size, Liechtenstein packs a punch when it comes to natural beauty and diversity.

The terrain of Liechtenstein is dominated by the majestic peaks of the Alps, which rise sharply from the valley floors to heights of over 2,000 meters. These towering mountains not only provide a stunning backdrop for the country's picturesque villages and towns but also offer ample opportunities for outdoor recreation, including hiking, skiing, and mountaineering. The highest point in Liechtenstein is the Grauspitz, standing at 2,599 meters above sea level, offering breathtaking views of the surrounding landscape.

Flowing through the valleys of Liechtenstein are several pristine rivers and streams, including the Rhine, which forms the western border of the principality. The Rhine River, one of Europe's major waterways, not only provides a scenic backdrop for leisurely walks and picnics but also serves as a vital lifeline for transportation and commerce.

In addition to its mountainous terrain and flowing rivers, Liechtenstein is also home to lush forests, verdant meadows, and fertile agricultural land. These natural resources not only contribute to the country's stunning scenery but also support a diverse array of flora and fauna, including native species such as edelweiss, ibex, and chamois.

Despite its landlocked location, Liechtenstein enjoys a temperate climate with warm summers and cold winters, thanks in part to its proximity to the Alps and the influence of the Atlantic Ocean. The climate varies depending on altitude, with lower elevations experiencing milder temperatures and higher elevations receiving heavier snowfall during the winter months.

Overall, Liechtenstein's geography is a testament to the beauty and diversity of the Alpine region, offering visitors and residents alike a wealth of natural wonders to explore and enjoy. From snow-capped peaks to rolling hillsides, from rushing rivers to tranquil valleys, Liechtenstein's landscape is a source of inspiration and awe, beckoning travelers to discover its hidden treasures and timeless charm.

Exploring Liechtenstein's Natural Beauty: Landscapes and Wildlife

Exploring Liechtenstein's natural beauty is an adventure that promises to delight the senses and nourish the soul. From its majestic Alpine peaks to its serene valleys and meandering rivers, the principality is a paradise for outdoor enthusiasts and nature lovers alike. The landscape of Liechtenstein is characterized by rugged mountains, verdant forests, and picturesque villages, creating a tapestry of colors and textures that captivates the imagination.

One of the most iconic features of Liechtenstein's natural landscape is its towering Alpine peaks, which dominate the skyline and offer panoramic views of the surrounding countryside. The Grauspitz, the highest peak in the principality, stands at an impressive 2,599 meters above sea level, beckoning adventurous hikers and mountaineers to conquer its summit and soak in the breathtaking vistas.

In addition to its mountains, Liechtenstein is also home to a network of scenic hiking trails that wind their way through forests, meadows, and alpine pastures. These well-marked paths offer hikers of all skill levels the opportunity to explore the countryside at their own pace, discovering hidden waterfalls, alpine lakes, and secluded mountain huts along the way.

The forests of Liechtenstein are teeming with life, providing habitat for a diverse array of plant and animal species. From towering conifers to delicate wildflowers, the flora of Liechtenstein is as varied as it is beautiful, with each season bringing its own kaleidoscope of colors and scents. Wildlife enthusiasts can spot native species such as red deer, roe deer, and European badgers roaming freely in their natural habitat, while birdwatchers can marvel at the sight of migratory birds soaring overhead.

The rivers and streams of Liechtenstein are another integral part of its natural landscape, offering opportunities for fishing, kayaking, and picnicking along their banks. The Rhine River, which forms the western border of the principality, is a popular spot for leisurely boat rides and scenic cruises, providing a unique perspective on the surrounding countryside.

Despite its small size, Liechtenstein boasts an impressive array of protected areas and nature reserves, dedicated to preserving its natural heritage for future generations to enjoy. These protected areas serve as sanctuaries for rare and endangered species, as well as havens for outdoor recreation and ecotourism.

Overall, exploring Liechtenstein's natural beauty is an enriching experience that fosters a deep connection with the land and its inhabitants. Whether scaling mountain peaks, wandering through forests, or paddling along tranquil rivers, there is no shortage of wonders to discover in this tiny Alpine principality.

Alpine Adventures: Outdoor Activities in Liechtenstein

Alpine adventures beckon in Liechtenstein, offering outdoor enthusiasts a playground of exhilarating activities amidst breathtaking natural beauty. Nestled in the heart of the Alps, this tiny principality boasts a wealth of opportunities for adventure seekers of all ages and skill levels. Whether scaling towering peaks, traversing scenic trails, or exploring tranquil valleys, there's something for everyone to enjoy in Liechtenstein's great outdoors.

Hiking is one of the most popular activities in Liechtenstein, with a vast network of well-marked trails crisscrossing the countryside. From leisurely strolls through picturesque villages to challenging ascents of rugged mountain peaks, hikers can explore a variety of landscapes and ecosystems, each offering its own unique charms and rewards. The Fürstensteig Trail, the Panoramaweg Trail, and the Alpweg Trail are just a few of the many options available to adventurous trekkers.

For those seeking a thrill, rock climbing provides an adrenaline-pumping challenge amidst the majestic cliffs and crags of the Alps. Liechtenstein offers numerous climbing routes suitable for climbers of all abilities, from beginner-friendly crags to advanced multi-pitch routes. The Falknis Climbing Area and the Grauspitz Massif are popular destinations for climbers looking to test their skills against the rugged terrain.

Cycling enthusiasts will find plenty to love in Liechtenstein, with a network of scenic cycling routes winding through the countryside. Whether mountain biking along rugged trails or leisurely pedaling through charming villages, cyclists can explore the principality at their own pace, soaking in the stunning scenery and fresh mountain air along the way. The Rhine Cycle Route, the Alpenrhein Route, and the Fürstenweg Trail are just a few of the options available to cyclists eager to explore Liechtenstein on two wheels.

In the winter months, Liechtenstein transforms into a winter wonderland, with opportunities for skiing, snowboarding, and snowshoeing abound. The Malbun Ski Resort, nestled in the heart of the Alps, offers pristine slopes and modern amenities for skiers and snowboarders of all levels. For those seeking a quieter experience, the region's network of cross-country ski trails provides a peaceful escape amidst the snow-covered landscape.

In addition to these activities, Liechtenstein also offers opportunities for paragliding, horseback riding, fishing, and more, ensuring that there's never a dull moment for outdoor enthusiasts in this Alpine paradise. Whether seeking an adrenaline rush or a moment of tranquility, visitors to Liechtenstein are sure to find their own slice of adventure amidst its stunning natural beauty.

Liechtenstein's Economic Success Story: From Agriculture to Finance

Liechtenstein's economic success story is a testament to its resilience, adaptability, and entrepreneurial spirit. Historically, the principality's economy was predominantly agrarian, with agriculture playing a central role in its early development. However, in the 20th century, Liechtenstein underwent a remarkable transformation, transitioning from agriculture to industry and finance.

The decline of traditional agriculture in Liechtenstein was driven by various factors, including changing market dynamics, technological advancements, and shifts in consumer preferences. As agricultural productivity waned, Liechtenstein's leaders recognized the need to diversify the economy and explore new avenues for growth.

One of the key turning points in Liechtenstein's economic history came in the aftermath of World War II, when the principality embraced industrialization and began to attract foreign investment. Leveraging its strategic location, skilled workforce, and business-friendly policies, Liechtenstein quickly became a hub for manufacturing, particularly in sectors such as electronics, textiles, and precision engineering.

However, it was the emergence of the financial services sector that truly propelled Liechtenstein onto the global stage. In the 1960s and 1970s, Liechtenstein capitalized on its reputation for stability, discretion, and favorable tax laws to attract foreign banks and financial institutions. The principality's banking sector flourished, offering a range of services including private banking, wealth management, and asset protection to clients from around the world.

Today, Liechtenstein's financial services industry is a cornerstone of its economy, contributing significantly to its GDP and providing employment opportunities for thousands of people. The principality is home to over 120 banks and financial intermediaries, managing assets worth billions of dollars on behalf of clients from every corner of the globe.

In addition to banking and finance, Liechtenstein has also diversified into other sectors such as tourism, technology, and healthcare. The principality's commitment to innovation and sustainability has attracted businesses and investors seeking to capitalize on its unique advantages and opportunities.

Despite its small size, Liechtenstein punches above its weight when it comes to economic competitiveness and prosperity. With a high standard of living, low unemployment rate, and robust social welfare system, the principality has earned a reputation as one of the wealthiest and most stable countries in the world.

Looking to the future, Liechtenstein continues to embrace innovation and entrepreneurship, investing in research and development, education, and infrastructure to ensure sustained economic growth and prosperity for generations to come. As it navigates the challenges and opportunities of the 21st century, Liechtenstein remains committed to its legacy of economic success and prosperity, forging ahead as a beacon of innovation and opportunity in the heart of Europe.

Vaduz: The Charming Capital City of Liechtenstein

Vaduz, the capital city of Liechtenstein, exudes charm and sophistication in equal measure. Situated in the Rhine Valley, this picturesque city is the beating heart of the tiny principality, serving as its political, cultural, and economic center. Despite its small size, Vaduz boasts a rich history and a vibrant contemporary scene that captivates visitors from around the world.

At the heart of Vaduz lies the iconic Vaduz Castle, perched atop a hill overlooking the city. Dating back to the 12th century, this medieval fortress serves as the official residence of the Prince of Liechtenstein and is a symbol of the principality's enduring heritage. While the castle itself is not open to the public, visitors can admire its picturesque silhouette and panoramic views of the surrounding countryside.

Descending from the castle, visitors find themselves in the charming old town of Vaduz, characterized by narrow cobblestone streets, historic buildings, and quaint cafes. The Rathaus, or Town Hall, is a focal point of the old town, with its distinctive neo-Gothic facade and clock tower serving as a landmark for locals and visitors alike.

Vaduz is also home to a vibrant arts and cultural scene, with numerous museums, galleries, and cultural institutions showcasing the best of

Liechtenstein's heritage and creativity. The Kunstmuseum Liechtenstein, housed in a striking modernist building, features a diverse collection of contemporary art from around the world, while the Liechtenstein National Museum offers insight into the principality's history and culture through interactive exhibits and artifacts.

For those seeking retail therapy, Vaduz offers a variety of shopping opportunities, from high-end boutiques and designer shops to quaint local markets and artisanal craft stores. The pedestrianized Städtle street is a shopper's paradise, lined with shops selling everything from luxury goods to traditional souvenirs.

Culinary enthusiasts will also find much to savor in Vaduz, with a diverse array of restaurants, cafes, and eateries serving up a mix of international cuisine and local specialties. From cozy family-run taverns serving hearty Alpine fare to upscale fine dining establishments offering gourmet delights, Vaduz has something to please every palate.

But perhaps the true charm of Vaduz lies in its warm and welcoming atmosphere, where locals and visitors mingle in the shadow of the castle, sharing stories, laughter, and a sense of community. Whether exploring its historic landmarks, soaking in its cultural riches, or simply strolling through its charming streets, Vaduz offers an unforgettable experience that leaves a lasting impression on all who visit.

Balzers: A Glimpse into Liechtenstein's Rural Charm

Nestled in the southernmost region of Liechtenstein lies the idyllic village of Balzers, a quintessential example of the principality's rural charm. With a population of just over 4,000 residents, Balzers is one of the largest municipalities in Liechtenstein, yet it retains a quaint and intimate atmosphere that harkens back to simpler times.

At the heart of Balzers lies the historic old town, characterized by traditional wooden chalets, rustic farmhouses, and quaint cobblestone streets. The village square, with its picturesque fountain and flower-filled gardens, serves as a gathering place for locals and visitors alike, offering a glimpse into everyday life in rural Liechtenstein.

One of the most iconic landmarks in Balzers is the medieval Gutenberg Castle, perched atop a rocky hill overlooking the village. Dating back to the 12th century, this majestic fortress is one of the best-preserved castles in Liechtenstein and offers panoramic views of the surrounding countryside. Visitors can explore the castle's interior, which houses a museum showcasing artifacts and exhibits related to the region's history and heritage.

In addition to its historic charm, Balzers is also known for its scenic natural beauty, with lush forests, rolling hills, and meandering rivers surrounding the village. Outdoor enthusiasts will find plenty to enjoy in the surrounding countryside, with hiking trails, cycling routes, and picnic spots aplenty.

For those interested in local culture and traditions, Balzers hosts a variety of festivals and events throughout the year, including traditional folk music performances, craft fairs, and seasonal celebrations. These events offer visitors the opportunity to immerse themselves in the rich cultural heritage of rural Liechtenstein and connect with the local community.

Despite its rural setting, Balzers is also home to modern amenities and conveniences, including shops, restaurants, and recreational facilities. The village's central location makes it an ideal base for exploring the rest of Liechtenstein, as well as nearby attractions in Switzerland and Austria.

But perhaps the true charm of Balzers lies in its warm and welcoming atmosphere, where neighbors greet each other with a smile and time seems to slow down just a little. Whether wandering through its historic streets, soaking in its natural beauty, or simply enjoying the company of its friendly residents, Balzers offers a glimpse into the heart and soul of rural Liechtenstein, a place where tradition and modernity coexist in perfect harmony.

Schaan: Industrial Hub and Cultural Center

Nestled in the northern region of Liechtenstein lies the dynamic town of Schaan, a bustling industrial hub and vibrant cultural center. With a population of over 6,000 residents, Schaan is the largest municipality in the principality and plays a pivotal role in its economic and cultural life.

At the heart of Schaan lies an industrial landscape dotted with factories, warehouses, and production facilities, making it a key center for manufacturing and commerce in Liechtenstein. The town's strategic location, nestled between the Rhine River and the foothills of the Alps, has attracted businesses from a variety of industries, including construction, engineering, and technology.

One of the most prominent features of Schaan's industrial landscape is the presence of international companies such as Hilti and Ivoclar Vivadent, which have their headquarters or major operations located in the town. These companies are leaders in their respective fields and contribute significantly to Schaan's economic prosperity and global reputation.

Despite its industrial character, Schaan is also a vibrant cultural center, with a rich array of artistic, musical, and recreational activities to enjoy. The town is home to several museums and galleries, including the Liechtensteinisches Landesmuseum, which showcases the history and culture of the principality through interactive exhibits and artifacts.

For those seeking outdoor recreation, Schaan offers numerous parks, gardens, and green spaces where residents and visitors can relax and unwind amidst the natural beauty of the Alpine landscape. The Unterland Trail, a scenic hiking route that winds its way through the countryside, offers stunning views of the Rhine Valley and surrounding mountains.

Cultural events and festivals abound in Schaan, with highlights including the Schaaner Festwochen, a summer festival featuring concerts, theater performances, and art exhibitions, as well as the Schaaner Märkli-Märt, a traditional market showcasing local crafts, food, and entertainment.

In addition to its industrial and cultural offerings, Schaan also boasts modern amenities and infrastructure, including shops, restaurants, schools, and recreational facilities. The town's central location makes it an ideal base for exploring the rest of Liechtenstein, as well as nearby attractions in Switzerland and Austria.

But perhaps the true charm of Schaan lies in its diverse and dynamic community, where residents from all walks of life come together to live, work, and play. Whether strolling through its industrial districts, exploring its cultural institutions, or simply enjoying the company of its friendly inhabitants, Schaan offers a unique blend of urban excitement and rural tranquility that is sure to leave a lasting impression on all who visit.

Triesen: A Historical Journey through Liechtenstein's Past

Triesen, nestled in the central region of Liechtenstein, is a town steeped in history, offering visitors a fascinating journey through the principality's past. With a history dating back over a thousand years, Triesen is one of the oldest settlements in Liechtenstein and has played a significant role in shaping the country's cultural and political landscape.

At the heart of Triesen lies its historic old town, characterized by narrow cobblestone streets, centuries-old buildings, and charming squares. The town's medieval roots are evident in its architecture, with landmarks such as the Church of St. Gallus, dating back to the 15th century, and the Schädlerhaus, a well-preserved example of traditional Liechtensteinian architecture.

One of the most iconic features of Triesen is the ruins of Schloss Vaduz, a medieval fortress perched atop a rocky hill overlooking the town. Built in the 12th century, the castle served as a strategic stronghold for the rulers of Liechtenstein and offers panoramic views of the surrounding countryside. Today, the ruins are a popular tourist attraction, drawing visitors from far and wide to explore its ancient walls and hidden passageways.

In addition to its medieval heritage, Triesen also boasts a rich agricultural tradition, with vineyards, orchards, and farms dotting the surrounding countryside. The town's fertile soil and favorable climate have long supported a thriving agricultural economy, producing a variety of crops including grapes, apples, and grains.

Triesen's location along the banks of the Rhine River has also played a significant role in its history and development. The river served as a vital artery for trade and transportation, allowing goods and people to flow freely between Liechtenstein and its neighbors. Today, the Rhine River continues to be an important lifeline for the town, offering opportunities for recreation and leisure activities such as boating, fishing, and riverside picnics.

Cultural events and festivals are a highlight of life in Triesen, with traditions such as the Triesenberg Alpabfahrt, a colorful celebration of the return of cattle from the Alpine pastures, and the Triesen Carnival, a lively street festival featuring music, dancing, and elaborate costumes.

Despite its rich history and cultural heritage, Triesen is also a modern and vibrant town, with modern amenities and infrastructure including shops, restaurants, and recreational facilities. Its central location makes it an ideal base for exploring the rest of Liechtenstein, as well as nearby attractions in Switzerland and Austria.

But perhaps the true charm of Triesen lies in its warm and welcoming atmosphere, where residents and visitors alike come together to celebrate the town's rich history and cultural heritage. Whether exploring its historic streets, sampling its local delicacies, or simply soaking in the breathtaking views of the Rhine Valley, Triesen offers a captivating glimpse into the past and present of Liechtenstein.

Mauren: Traditions and Modernity Intertwined

Nestled in the northeastern region of Liechtenstein lies the charming village of Mauren, where traditions and modernity intertwine to create a unique and vibrant community. With a population of over 4,000 residents, Mauren is one of the smaller municipalities in the principality, yet it boasts a rich cultural heritage and a dynamic contemporary scene that captivates visitors from near and far.

At the heart of Mauren lies its historic old town, characterized by traditional timber-framed houses, cobblestone streets, and quaint village squares. The village's medieval roots are evident in its architecture, with landmarks such as the Parish Church of St. Martin, dating back to the 13th century, and the Alte Landbrugg, a historic bridge spanning the Rhine River.

But while Mauren's history is deeply rooted in tradition, the village is also a modern and forward-thinking community, with a strong emphasis on innovation and sustainability. In recent years, Mauren has implemented a variety of green initiatives, including renewable energy projects, waste reduction programs, and eco-friendly transportation options, earning it recognition as a leader in environmental stewardship.

Cultural events and festivals are an integral part of life in Mauren, with traditions such as the Mauren

Dorffest, a lively street festival featuring music, dancing, and local cuisine, and the Mauren Ländlefest, a celebration of Liechtenstein's rural heritage, drawing residents and visitors alike to come together and celebrate.

In addition to its cultural offerings, Mauren is also home to modern amenities and conveniences, including shops, restaurants, and recreational facilities. The village's central location makes it an ideal base for exploring the rest of Liechtenstein, as well as nearby attractions in Switzerland and Austria.

One of the most striking features of Mauren is its natural beauty, with lush forests, rolling hills, and meandering rivers surrounding the village. Outdoor enthusiasts will find plenty to enjoy in the surrounding countryside, with hiking trails, cycling routes, and picnic spots aplenty.

But perhaps the true charm of Mauren lies in its warm and welcoming atmosphere, where neighbors greet each other with a smile and time seems to slow down just a little. Whether strolling through its historic streets, exploring its cultural institutions, or simply enjoying the company of its friendly inhabitants, Mauren offers a unique blend of tradition and modernity that is sure to leave a lasting impression on all who visit.

The Rich Cultural Tapestry of Liechtenstein: Arts and Festivals

Liechtenstein's cultural tapestry is rich and diverse, woven from centuries of tradition, innovation, and creativity. At the heart of this tapestry lies a vibrant arts scene, where artists, musicians, and performers come together to express themselves and share their talents with the world. From traditional folk music and dance to contemporary art exhibitions and theatrical performances, Liechtenstein offers a wealth of cultural experiences for residents and visitors alike to enjoy.

One of the highlights of Liechtenstein's cultural calendar is the Schaaner Festwochen, a summer festival that celebrates the arts in all its forms. This month-long extravaganza features a diverse lineup of concerts, theater productions, film screenings, and art exhibitions, attracting artists and audiences from around the world. Whether you're a fan of classical music, jazz, or rock and roll, there's something for everyone to enjoy at the Schaaner Festwochen.

But the cultural scene in Liechtenstein isn't limited to just one town or one festival. Throughout the year, communities across the principality come alive with a variety of cultural events and celebrations. From the Triesen Carnival, a colorful street festival featuring elaborate costumes and lively music, to the Mauren Ländlefest, a celebration of Liechtenstein's rural heritage complete with traditional food, music, and dancing, there's always something exciting happening in Liechtenstein.

In addition to its festivals and events, Liechtenstein also boasts a thriving arts community, with numerous galleries, museums, and cultural institutions showcasing the work of local and international artists. The Kunstmuseum Liechtenstein, housed in a striking modernist building in Vaduz, features a diverse collection of contemporary art from around the world, while the Liechtenstein National Museum offers insight into the principality's history and culture through interactive exhibits and artifacts.

But perhaps the most cherished cultural tradition in Liechtenstein is the Alpabfahrt, or Alpine descent, a centuries-old tradition that marks the end of the summer grazing season. During the Alpabfahrt, farmers decorate their cattle with elaborate floral headdresses and lead them down from the Alpine pastures to the valleys below, where they are greeted with music, food, and festivities. This colorful and festive celebration is a testament to Liechtenstein's rural heritage and the close connection between its people and the land.

Overall, Liechtenstein's cultural tapestry is as diverse and vibrant as the people who call it home. Whether you're exploring its museums and galleries, attending its festivals and events, or simply soaking in the sights and sounds of everyday life, Liechtenstein offers a cultural experience that is both rich in tradition and brimming with creativity.

Liechtenstein's Culinary Delights: A Fusion of Alpine and International Flavors

Liechtenstein's culinary scene is a delightful fusion of Alpine traditions and international influences, offering a diverse array of flavors and dishes to tantalize the taste buds. At the heart of Liechtenstein's cuisine lies a deep appreciation for fresh, locally sourced ingredients, with a focus on quality, simplicity, and flavor.

One of the most iconic dishes in Liechtenstein is käsknöpfle, a hearty pasta dish similar to Austrian käsespätzle or Swiss käseknöpfli. Made with small dumplings of pasta cooked in a creamy cheese sauce and topped with crispy onions, käsknöpfle is a comforting and satisfying meal that is beloved by locals and visitors alike.

Another popular dish in Liechtenstein is rösti, a crispy potato pancake that originated in Switzerland but has become a staple of Alpine cuisine. Served as a side dish or as a main course topped with cheese, bacon, or fried eggs, rösti is a versatile and delicious addition to any meal.

For meat lovers, Liechtenstein offers a variety of hearty dishes featuring locally sourced meats such as pork, beef, and game. One traditional dish is geschnetzeltes, thinly sliced meat cooked in a rich, creamy sauce and served with noodles or potatoes. Other popular meat dishes include bratwurst, a type of sausage served with sauerkraut and mustard, and venison stew, made with tender chunks of deer meat simmered in a flavorful broth. Seafood lovers will also find plenty to enjoy in Liechtenstein, with dishes featuring freshwater fish such as trout and perch caught in the pristine rivers and lakes of the Alps. Grilled trout with herb butter, smoked perch salad, and fish soup are just a few examples of the delicious seafood offerings available in Liechtenstein.

No meal in Liechtenstein would be complete without dessert, and the principality offers a tempting array of sweet treats to satisfy any sweet tooth. One popular dessert is apfelstrudel, a flaky pastry filled with cinnamon-spiced apples and served with whipped cream or vanilla sauce. Other favorites include kirschplotzer, a cherry tart made with a buttery pastry crust, and rüebli cake, a moist carrot cake topped with cream cheese frosting.

To wash it all down, Liechtenstein offers a variety of beverages ranging from local wines and beers to herbal liqueurs and fruit schnapps. The principality's wine industry has been gaining recognition in recent years, with vineyards producing high-quality white and red wines from grapes grown in the fertile Rhine Valley.

Overall, Liechtenstein's culinary delights are a reflection of its rich cultural heritage and diverse landscape, offering a taste of Alpine tradition with a modern twist. Whether dining in a cozy mountain chalet, a traditional tavern, or a gourmet restaurant, visitors to Liechtenstein are sure to be delighted by the delicious flavors and warm hospitality of this charming principality.

Winegrowing in Liechtenstein: A Tradition of Quality and Excellence

Winegrowing in Liechtenstein is a tradition that dates back centuries, rooted in the fertile soils of the Rhine Valley and nurtured by a favorable climate and a commitment to quality and excellence. Despite its small size, Liechtenstein boasts a thriving wine industry that has earned recognition for its exceptional wines and dedication to craftsmanship.

The history of winegrowing in Liechtenstein can be traced back to Roman times, when vines were first cultivated in the region. Over the centuries, the art of winemaking has been passed down from generation to generation, with families and winemakers honing their skills and refining their techniques to produce wines of unparalleled quality.

Today, Liechtenstein is home to several dozen wineries and vineyards, each with its own unique terroir and varietals. The principality's diverse microclimates, ranging from the warm, sunny slopes of the Rhine Valley to the cooler, higher-altitude vineyards in the mountains, offer ideal conditions for growing a variety of grape varietals, including Pinot Noir, Chardonnay, and Riesling.

One of the most renowned wine regions in Liechtenstein is the Prince of Liechtenstein Winery, located in Vaduz. Established in the 18th century, this historic winery is one of the oldest in the principality and is known for producing award-winning wines that showcase the unique character of Liechtenstein's terroir.

In addition to the Prince of Liechtenstein Winery, there are numerous other wineries and vineyards scattered throughout the principality, each contributing to Liechtenstein's reputation as a premier winegrowing region. From small, family-owned estates to larger, commercial operations, these winemakers share a common passion for their craft and a commitment to producing wines of exceptional quality.

Despite its small size, Liechtenstein's wine industry punches above its weight on the international stage, with its wines earning accolades and awards at prestigious competitions around the world. The principality's wines are prized for their purity, finesse, and expression of terroir, reflecting the dedication and expertise of the winemakers who produce them.

In recent years, Liechtenstein's wine industry has undergone a renaissance, with a new generation of winemakers embracing innovation and sustainability to further elevate the quality of their wines. From organic and biodynamic farming practices to state-of-the-art winemaking techniques, Liechtenstein's winemakers are committed to preserving the natural beauty of their vineyards and crafting wines that are true expressions of the land.

Overall, winegrowing in Liechtenstein is more than just a tradition—it's a way of life. From the vineyards that carpet the hillsides to the cellars where wines are aged and bottled, every aspect of the winemaking process is infused with a sense of pride, passion, and respect for the land. As Liechtenstein's wine industry continues to evolve and flourish, it remains a shining example of the principality's commitment to quality, excellence, and the pursuit of perfection in every glass.

The Language of Liechtenstein: A Blend of German Dialects

The language of Liechtenstein is predominantly German, specifically a blend of Alemannic dialects spoken in the region. This Germanic language is the official language of the principality and is used in government, education, and everyday communication. However, Liechtenstein's proximity to Switzerland and Austria means that there are also influences from Swiss German and Austrian German dialects in the local language.

The Alemannic dialect spoken in Liechtenstein shares many similarities with the dialects spoken in neighboring regions of Switzerland and Austria, but it also has its own unique characteristics and vocabulary. For example, certain words and expressions may be specific to Liechtenstein or have slightly different meanings than they do in other German-speaking regions.

Despite the prevalence of German in Liechtenstein, the principality is also home to a diverse population of people from various cultural backgrounds, leading to a multilingual society where other languages are also spoken. English is widely understood and spoken, particularly among younger generations and in business and tourism settings. Additionally, many residents of Liechtenstein also speak Swiss German or Austrian German, particularly those who have family ties or business connections in those countries.

In recent years, efforts have been made to preserve and promote the Alemannic dialects spoken in Liechtenstein, particularly among younger generations. Organizations and cultural institutions have launched initiatives to document and celebrate the local language, including language courses, cultural events, and publications in the dialect.

Overall, the language of Liechtenstein reflects the principality's rich cultural heritage and its close ties to neighboring German-speaking countries. While German is the dominant language, the influence of Swiss and Austrian dialects adds depth and diversity to the linguistic landscape, creating a unique and vibrant linguistic identity for this small but dynamic nation.

Education in Liechtenstein: Nurturing Minds in a Principality

Education in Liechtenstein is highly valued and is considered a cornerstone of the principality's success and development. The education system in Liechtenstein is comprehensive, providing students with a well-rounded education from early childhood through higher education.

Early childhood education in Liechtenstein begins with kindergarten, which is available to children from the age of four. Kindergartens in Liechtenstein focus on providing a nurturing and stimulating environment where children can develop social, emotional, and cognitive skills through play-based learning activities.

Primary education in Liechtenstein is compulsory for all children between the ages of six and nine. Primary schools in Liechtenstein offer a curriculum that includes subjects such as mathematics, science, languages, and the arts. The primary education system in Liechtenstein is designed to provide students with a solid foundation in core academic subjects while also fostering creativity, critical thinking, and social skills.

After completing primary education, students in Liechtenstein move on to secondary education, which is divided into lower secondary and upper secondary levels. Lower secondary education, also known as Sekundarschule, lasts for four years and is followed by upper secondary education, which includes a variety of vocational and academic pathways.

One of the unique features of Liechtenstein's education system is its dual system of vocational and academic education. Students in Liechtenstein have the option to pursue vocational training in a variety of fields, including engineering, healthcare, and business, through apprenticeships or vocational schools. Alternatively, students can choose to pursue an academic track that prepares them for higher education.

Higher education in Liechtenstein is provided primarily by the University of Liechtenstein, which offers undergraduate and graduate programs in business administration, architecture, and law, among other fields. In addition to the University of Liechtenstein, there are also several vocational schools and professional training institutes that offer specialized training and education programs in various fields.

The education system in Liechtenstein is overseen by the Ministry of Education, which is responsible for setting educational standards, curriculum development, and teacher training. The government of Liechtenstein is committed to providing a high-quality education for all residents of the principality and invests heavily in education and training programs to ensure that students have access to the knowledge and skills they need to succeed in an increasingly globalized world.

The Liechtensteinische Landesmuseum: Preserving the Nation's Heritage

The Liechtensteinische Landesmuseum, or the National Museum of Liechtenstein, stands as a beacon of the principality's rich cultural heritage, dedicated to preserving and showcasing the nation's history, art, and culture. Situated in the heart of Vaduz, the capital city, the museum is housed in a striking modern building that reflects Liechtenstein's commitment to innovation and tradition.

The history of the Liechtensteinische Landesmuseum dates back to the late 19th century when it was founded as the National Museum of Liechtenstein in 1895. Over the years, the museum has grown and expanded its collections, acquiring artifacts, artworks, and archival materials that offer insight into the history and culture of Liechtenstein.

Today, the Liechtensteinische Landesmuseum boasts a diverse collection that spans centuries, from prehistoric artifacts to contemporary artworks. The museum's permanent exhibitions cover a wide range of topics, including archaeology, history, folk art, and natural history, providing visitors with a comprehensive overview of Liechtenstein's cultural heritage.

One of the highlights of the Liechtensteinische Landesmuseum is its collection of artifacts from the Middle Ages, including medieval manuscripts, religious artifacts, and decorative arts. These artifacts offer a glimpse into life in Liechtenstein during the Middle Ages and shed light on the principality's cultural and religious traditions.

In addition to its permanent exhibitions, the Liechtensteinische Landesmuseum also hosts temporary exhibitions, special events, and educational programs throughout the year. These events offer visitors the opportunity to delve deeper into specific aspects of Liechtenstein's history and culture and engage with experts and scholars in the field.

The Liechtensteinische Landesmuseum also plays an important role in research and scholarship, with its collections serving as valuable resources for historians, archaeologists, and other scholars studying Liechtenstein's past. The museum's library and archives house a wealth of materials related to the principality's history and culture, including rare books, manuscripts, and documents.

But perhaps the most important role of the Liechtensteinische Landesmuseum is its role in preserving and safeguarding Liechtenstein's cultural heritage for future generations. Through its exhibitions, programs, and outreach efforts, the museum ensures that the history and culture of Liechtenstein are not forgotten but rather celebrated and cherished for years to come.

Vaduz Castle: The Iconic Symbol of Liechtenstein

Vaduz Castle stands proudly atop a rocky hill overlooking the capital city of Vaduz, serving as the iconic symbol of Liechtenstein's rich history and heritage. This majestic fortress has a history that stretches back over 700 years, making it one of the oldest landmarks in the principality.

The origins of Vaduz Castle can be traced back to the 12th century when it was built as a medieval fortress by the Counts of Werdenberg. Over the centuries, the castle underwent several renovations and expansions, evolving from a simple defensive structure into the impressive Renaissance-style residence that stands today.

One of the most notable features of Vaduz Castle is its distinctive red-tiled roof and whitewashed walls, which give it a striking appearance against the backdrop of the surrounding mountains. The castle's commanding position atop the hill offers panoramic views of the Rhine Valley, making it a popular destination for visitors seeking to take in the beauty of the principality's landscape.

While Vaduz Castle has served various purposes throughout its long history, including as a residence for the ruling family and a military stronghold, today it serves primarily as a symbol of Liechtenstein's sovereignty and cultural heritage. The castle is still owned by the princely family of

Liechtenstein, who occasionally use it for official functions and events.

Despite its historic significance, Vaduz Castle is not open to the public for tours or visits. However, visitors to Liechtenstein can still admire the castle from the outside and take in its impressive architecture and breathtaking views. Additionally, the castle's grounds are occasionally used for special events and celebrations, adding to its allure as a symbol of national pride.

Vaduz Castle is also featured prominently on Liechtenstein's coat of arms and official seals, further cementing its status as a symbol of the principality's identity and heritage. Whether seen from afar or up close, Vaduz Castle continues to capture the imagination of visitors and residents alike, serving as a timeless reminder of Liechtenstein's rich history and enduring legacy.

The Princely Collection: Art Treasures of Liechtenstein's Rulers

The Princely Collection stands as a testament to the rich cultural legacy of Liechtenstein's rulers, housing one of the most extensive and valuable private art collections in the world. With roots dating back over five centuries, the collection encompasses a diverse array of artworks spanning various periods, styles, and mediums.

Originally assembled by the princely family of Liechtenstein, the collection includes paintings, sculptures, decorative arts, and other treasures acquired over generations through purchases, commissions, and inheritance. Many of the artworks in the collection were acquired by members of the princely family during the Renaissance and Baroque periods, reflecting their passion for art and patronage of the arts.

One of the highlights of the Princely Collection is its impressive collection of Old Master paintings, including works by renowned artists such as Peter Paul Rubens, Rembrandt van Rijn, and Leonardo da Vinci. These masterpieces offer insight into the artistic achievements of past centuries and showcase the princely family's discerning taste and connoisseurship.

In addition to its Old Master paintings, the Princely Collection also features significant holdings of European decorative arts, including furniture, ceramics, textiles, and silverware. These objects provide a glimpse into the princely lifestyle and the artistic and cultural trends of the time.

The collection's holdings have continued to grow and evolve over the years, with subsequent generations of the princely family adding to its riches through acquisitions and donations. Today, the Princely Collection is housed primarily in the Liechtenstein Museum in Vienna, Austria, where it is open to the public for viewing.

In recent years, the Princely Collection has expanded its focus to include contemporary art, reflecting the princely family's commitment to supporting and promoting emerging artists and innovative artistic practices. The collection's contemporary holdings include works by leading artists from around the world, as well as pieces commissioned specifically for the collection.

In addition to its role as a repository of artistic treasures, the Princely Collection also serves as a cultural ambassador for Liechtenstein, showcasing the principality's rich cultural heritage and artistic achievements to audiences around the world. Through exhibitions, loans, and collaborations with museums and cultural institutions, the Princely Collection continues to foster appreciation for art and culture while preserving the legacy of Liechtenstein's rulers for future generations to enjoy.

Gutenberg Castle: A Medieval Marvel in Liechtenstein

Gutenberg Castle stands as a medieval marvel perched atop a rocky hill in the town of Balzers, Liechtenstein. Its origins trace back to the High Middle Ages, with the earliest records of the castle dating back to the 12th century. Originally built as a fortress to defend the region, Gutenberg Castle has undergone numerous renovations and expansions over the centuries, evolving into the formidable stronghold that we see today.

The castle takes its name from Johannes Gutenberg, the inventor of the printing press, who is said to have been born in the castle or nearby. While there is debate among historians about the exact location of Gutenberg's birth, the castle remains closely associated with his legacy, serving as a symbol of innovation and cultural significance.

Gutenberg Castle is characterized by its sturdy stone walls, imposing towers, and commanding position overlooking the Rhine Valley. From its strategic vantage point, the castle offers panoramic views of the surrounding countryside, making it both a defensive stronghold and a picturesque landmark.

Throughout its long history, Gutenberg Castle has served various purposes, including as a residence for noble families, a military garrison, and even a prison at one point. Over time, the castle fell into disrepair, but efforts have been made in recent years to restore and preserve this historic landmark for future generations to enjoy.

Today, Gutenberg Castle is open to the public for guided tours, allowing visitors to explore its medieval architecture, learn about its fascinating history, and take in the breathtaking views from its battlements. The castle also hosts cultural events, concerts, and exhibitions throughout the year, adding to its appeal as a tourist destination and cultural hub.

In addition to its historical and cultural significance, Gutenberg Castle is also home to the Liechtenstein State Museum, which showcases exhibits on the history, art, and culture of Liechtenstein. The museum's collections include artifacts, artworks, and archaeological finds that offer insight into the principality's rich heritage and cultural identity.

Overall, Gutenberg Castle stands as a testament to the resilience and ingenuity of the people of Liechtenstein, preserving the legacy of the past while embracing the opportunities of the future. As a medieval marvel and cultural landmark, the castle continues to captivate visitors and residents alike, inviting them to step back in time and explore the rich tapestry of Liechtenstein's history and heritage.

St. Florin Cathedral: Religious Heritage in Liechtenstein

St. Florin Cathedral stands as a towering symbol of religious heritage in Liechtenstein, its spires reaching towards the heavens as a testament to centuries of faith and devotion. Situated in the heart of Vaduz, the capital city, the cathedral is dedicated to Saint Florin, the patron saint of Liechtenstein, and serves as the spiritual center of the principality.

The history of St. Florin Cathedral can be traced back to the early 19th century when the original church on the site was demolished to make way for a larger, grander cathedral befitting the growing population of Vaduz. Construction of the new cathedral began in 1868 and was completed in 1873, with the consecration ceremony taking place in the presence of Prince Johann II of Liechtenstein.

Architecturally, St. Florin Cathedral is a fine example of neo-Gothic design, with its pointed arches, ribbed vaults, and intricate stained glass windows evoking the grandeur and splendor of medieval cathedrals. The cathedral's facade is adorned with statues of saints and religious motifs, while its interior features ornate altars, sculptures, and paintings depicting scenes from the life of Christ and the saints.

One of the most striking features of St. Florin Cathedral is its impressive organ, which was installed in 1961 and is renowned for its rich tone and exquisite craftsmanship. The organ is used regularly for concerts, recitals, and worship services, adding to the cathedral's reputation as a center of musical excellence in Liechtenstein.

In addition to its architectural and artistic significance, St. Florin Cathedral holds a special place in the hearts of the people of Liechtenstein as a place of worship, prayer, and spiritual reflection. The cathedral's doors are open to all, regardless of faith or denomination, and it welcomes visitors from around the world to experience its beauty and serenity.

Throughout its long history, St. Florin Cathedral has been a witness to many significant moments in the life of the principality, including royal weddings, state funerals, and religious ceremonies. Today, it continues to play an important role in the cultural and spiritual life of Liechtenstein, serving as a beacon of hope, inspiration, and unity for generations to come.

The Kunstmuseum Liechtenstein: Contemporary Art in a Historical Setting

The Kunstmuseum Liechtenstein stands as a vibrant cultural institution in the heart of Vaduz, the capital city of Liechtenstein, blending contemporary art with a historical setting to create a dynamic and engaging cultural experience. Established in 2000, the museum is housed in a striking modern building designed by Swiss architect Meinrad Morger, which complements the surrounding historic architecture while also making a bold architectural statement of its own.

The Kunstmuseum Liechtenstein is dedicated to showcasing contemporary art from around the world, with a particular focus on modern and contemporary art from Europe and beyond. The museum's collections include works in various mediums, including painting, sculpture, photography, video, and installation art, providing visitors with a diverse and eclectic range of artistic expressions to explore.

One of the highlights of the Kunstmuseum Liechtenstein is its collection of works by modern and contemporary artists, including pieces by renowned artists such as Gerhard Richter, Roy Lichtenstein, and Cindy Sherman. These artworks offer insight into the artistic movements and trends of the 20th and 21st centuries, as well as the cultural and social issues that have shaped the world we live in today.

In addition to its permanent collections, the Kunstmuseum Liechtenstein also hosts temporary exhibitions, special events, and educational programs throughout the year. These events offer visitors the opportunity to engage with contemporary art in new and innovative ways, whether through guided tours, artist talks, or hands-on workshops.

The museum's location in Vaduz, nestled amid the picturesque landscapes of the Rhine Valley, adds to its appeal as a cultural destination, attracting visitors from near and far to experience its world-class exhibitions and stunning architecture. The museum also plays an important role in the cultural life of Liechtenstein, serving as a hub for artistic expression, dialogue, and collaboration within the principality and beyond.

Overall, the Kunstmuseum Liechtenstein embodies the spirit of creativity, innovation, and exploration, inviting visitors to immerse themselves in the world of contemporary art while also celebrating the rich cultural heritage of Liechtenstein. As a beacon of artistic excellence in a historical setting, the museum continues to inspire and captivate audiences, fostering appreciation for the arts and culture in Liechtenstein and beyond.

Skiing in Malbun: Winter Sports Paradise in Liechtenstein

Nestled in the picturesque Alps of Liechtenstein, Malbun stands as a winter sports paradise, drawing skiers and snowboarders from near and far to its pristine slopes and breathtaking scenery. Situated at an elevation of over 1600 meters above sea level, Malbun offers ideal conditions for winter sports enthusiasts of all levels, from beginners to seasoned pros.

The ski resort in Malbun boasts a variety of slopes catering to different skill levels, including gentle beginner slopes for those just starting out, as well as challenging black diamond runs for the more experienced skiers and snowboarders. With over 23 kilometers of groomed pistes, there's plenty of terrain to explore, ensuring that every day on the slopes is filled with excitement and adventure.

In addition to downhill skiing and snowboarding, Malbun also offers a range of other winter activities, including cross-country skiing, snowshoeing, and tobogganing. The resort's well-maintained trails and scenic vistas make it the perfect destination for outdoor enthusiasts looking to enjoy the beauty of the Alps in winter.

For those seeking instruction or guidance on the slopes, Malbun has a number of ski schools and rental shops where visitors can book lessons, rent equipment, and get expert advice from certified instructors. Whether you're a first-time skier or looking to improve your technique, the friendly and knowledgeable staff at Malbun's ski schools are there to help you make the most of your time on the mountain.

After a day of skiing or snowboarding, visitors to Malbun can unwind and relax in the village's cozy cafes, restaurants, and apres-ski bars. Here, you can enjoy hearty alpine cuisine, warm up with a hot drink, or simply soak in the atmosphere as you recount the day's adventures with friends and family.

Beyond the slopes, Malbun offers a range of accommodations to suit every taste and budget, from luxury hotels and chalets to cozy guesthouses and mountain huts. Whether you're looking for a romantic getaway or a family-friendly retreat, you'll find plenty of options to choose from in this charming alpine village.

In conclusion, Malbun is much more than just a ski resort—it's a winter wonderland waiting to be explored. With its stunning scenery, diverse terrain, and warm hospitality, Malbun offers an unforgettable winter sports experience for visitors of all ages and abilities. So pack your skis or snowboard and head to Malbun for the ultimate winter adventure in Liechtenstein.

The Walser Museum: Exploring Liechtenstein's Alpine Heritage

The Walser Museum stands as a testament to Liechtenstein's rich Alpine heritage, offering visitors a fascinating glimpse into the history, culture, and traditions of the Walser people who settled in the region centuries ago. Located in the picturesque village of Triesenberg, the museum is housed in a charming historic building that once served as a traditional Walser farmhouse, adding to its authenticity and charm.

The Walser people were a Germanic-speaking group who migrated from the Swiss canton of Valais to the Alps of Liechtenstein and neighboring regions in the Middle Ages. Known for their distinct language, customs, and way of life, the Walser played a significant role in shaping the cultural landscape of the Alps and leaving their mark on the communities they inhabited.

The Walser Museum offers a comprehensive overview of Walser history and culture, with exhibits that showcase artifacts, photographs, documents, and interactive displays that bring the story of the Walser people to life. Visitors can learn about the daily life of the Walser, including their agricultural practices, crafts, religious traditions, and social customs, as well as their contributions to the development of the Alpine region.

One of the highlights of the Walser Museum is its collection of traditional Walser costumes, textiles, and handicrafts, which provide insight into the craftsmanship and artistic skills of the Walser people. From intricately embroidered garments to finely woven textiles, these artifacts offer a glimpse into the craftsmanship and artistry that have been passed down through generations.

In addition to its permanent exhibits, the Walser Museum also hosts special events, workshops, and educational programs throughout the year, offering visitors the opportunity to engage with Walser culture in a hands-on and immersive way. Whether participating in a traditional folk dance workshop or trying their hand at weaving on a loom, visitors can experience firsthand the richness and diversity of Walser heritage.

The Walser Museum also serves as a research center for scholars and historians studying the history and culture of the Walser people, with its library and archives housing a wealth of materials related to Walser history, linguistics, and ethnography. Researchers and enthusiasts alike can delve into the museum's collections to uncover new insights into this fascinating and resilient Alpine community.

Overall, the Walser Museum is a must-visit destination for anyone interested in exploring Liechtenstein's Alpine heritage and learning more about the vibrant culture of the Walser people. With its engaging exhibits, educational programs, and authentic setting, the museum offers a unique and enriching experience that celebrates the legacy of the Walser and their enduring influence on the Alpine region.

Liechtenstein's Banking Sector: A Pillar of Stability

Liechtenstein's banking sector has long been recognized as a pillar of stability and a key contributor to the principality's economy. Despite its small size, Liechtenstein has developed a robust and sophisticated banking industry that has earned a reputation for reliability, discretion, and financial expertise.

The origins of Liechtenstein's banking sector can be traced back to the early 20th century when the principality established favorable banking laws and regulations to attract foreign investment and capital. These laws, combined with Liechtenstein's political stability and geographical location, laid the foundation for the growth and development of the banking industry.

One of the key factors contributing to the success of Liechtenstein's banking sector is its tradition of banking secrecy and client confidentiality. Liechtenstein's banks are known for their strict adherence to confidentiality laws, which protect the privacy of their clients and ensure the security of their financial assets.

In addition to banking secrecy, Liechtenstein's banking sector offers a range of financial services to clients around the world, including private banking, wealth management, asset protection, and corporate banking. The principality's banks are known for their expertise in handling complex financial transactions and providing personalized services tailored to the needs of their clients.

Liechtenstein's banking sector has also benefited from its close proximity to major financial centers in Europe, such as Switzerland and Austria, allowing it to tap into international markets and attract a diverse clientele. Many multinational corporations, wealthy individuals, and family offices choose to bank in Liechtenstein due to its favorable tax environment, stable political climate, and reputation for reliability.

Despite its success, Liechtenstein's banking sector has faced challenges in recent years, including increased regulatory scrutiny and international pressure to improve transparency and combat financial crime. In response, the principality has implemented various reforms to strengthen its anti-money laundering and anti-terrorism financing measures, enhance regulatory oversight, and improve cooperation with international authorities.

Overall, Liechtenstein's banking sector remains a cornerstone of the principality's economy, contributing significantly to its GDP and providing employment opportunities for its citizens. With its commitment to excellence, integrity, and innovation, Liechtenstein's banks continue to play a vital role in the global financial landscape, helping to safeguard the wealth and assets of clients while supporting economic growth and prosperity in the principality.

The Liechtenstein Institute: Promoting Research and Dialogue

The Liechtenstein Institute stands as a beacon of intellectual inquiry and dialogue, dedicated to promoting research, scholarship, and discourse on matters of significance to Liechtenstein and the wider international community. Established in 1986, the institute serves as a hub for academic research, policy analysis, and public engagement, fostering collaboration between scholars, policymakers, and practitioners from around the world.

Located in the heart of Vaduz, Liechtenstein's capital city, the institute is affiliated with the University of Liechtenstein and operates as an independent research organization. Its mission is to generate knowledge, stimulate critical thinking, and facilitate informed debate on a wide range of topics, including politics, economics, law, history, and culture.

The Liechtenstein Institute conducts research on issues of relevance to Liechtenstein's society and economy, as well as broader global challenges facing the international community. Its interdisciplinary approach brings together experts from various fields and disciplines to explore complex issues from multiple perspectives, fostering innovative solutions and new insights.

One of the institute's key functions is to serve as a platform for dialogue and exchange, bringing together policymakers, academics, business leaders, and civil society representatives to discuss pressing issues and explore opportunities for collaboration. Through conferences, seminars, workshops, and public lectures, the institute provides a forum for informed debate and constructive dialogue on topics of mutual interest and concern.

In addition to its research and dialogue activities, the Liechtenstein Institute also publishes scholarly publications, policy papers, and research reports, disseminating its findings to a wider audience and contributing to the body of knowledge on Liechtenstein and related areas of inquiry. Its publications are widely recognized for their rigor, quality, and relevance to policymakers, academics, and practitioners alike.

The institute also engages in outreach and educational activities, collaborating with schools, universities, and community organizations to promote awareness and understanding of key issues facing Liechtenstein and the world. Through its educational programs, internships, and student exchanges, the institute seeks to inspire the next generation of leaders and scholars to make a positive impact on society.

Overall, the Liechtenstein Institute plays a vital role in advancing knowledge, fostering dialogue, and promoting understanding in Liechtenstein and beyond. As a trusted source of expertise and analysis, the institute contributes to informed decision-making, strengthens democratic governance, and enhances the principality's reputation as a center of excellence in research and scholarship.

The Philately Museum: A Stamp Collector's Haven

The Philately Museum, nestled in the heart of Vaduz, is a haven for stamp collectors and enthusiasts alike. Founded in 1930, it boasts a rich collection of stamps from around the world, spanning centuries of postal history and showcasing the artistry, culture, and heritage of nations near and far.

Walking into the Philately Museum is like stepping into a treasure trove of philatelic wonders. The museum's exhibits feature rare and valuable stamps, first-day covers, postal artifacts, and philatelic memorabilia, offering visitors a glimpse into the fascinating world of stamp collecting.

One of the museum's most prized possessions is the famed Blue Mauritius stamp, one of the rarest and most sought-after stamps in the world. Printed in 1847 in Mauritius, this iconic stamp is renowned for its distinctive blue color and exquisite design, making it a coveted item among collectors worldwide.

In addition to the Blue Mauritius, the Philately Museum houses an extensive collection of stamps from Liechtenstein, showcasing the principality's rich philatelic heritage and its contributions to the world of stamp collecting. From commemorative issues celebrating national milestones to thematic stamps highlighting the country's natural beauty and cultural heritage, Liechtenstein's stamps offer a window into its history, identity, and values.

The Philately Museum also hosts special exhibitions, events, and workshops throughout the year, providing visitors with opportunities to learn more about stamp collecting, philatelic history, and related topics. Whether attending a lecture by a renowned philatelist, participating in a hands-on workshop on stamp preservation, or browsing the latest additions to the museum's collection, visitors can immerse themselves in the world of philately and expand their knowledge and appreciation of stamps.

Beyond its role as a museum, the Philately Museum also serves as a research center and educational resource for philatelists, historians, and scholars interested in the study of stamps and postal history. Its library and archives house a wealth of materials, including books, journals, catalogs, and archival documents, providing a valuable source of information and inspiration for researchers and enthusiasts alike.

Overall, the Philately Museum is a must-visit destination for anyone with a passion for stamps and postal history. With its diverse collections, engaging exhibits, and educational programs, the museum offers a unique and immersive experience that celebrates the art, culture, and heritage of stamp collecting. Whether you're a seasoned collector or a curious novice, the Philately Museum invites you to explore the world of stamps and discover the stories they tell.

Liechtenstein National Library: A Treasure Trove of Knowledge

The Liechtenstein National Library stands as a bastion of knowledge and culture, preserving centuries of literary, historical, and cultural heritage for the people of Liechtenstein and visitors from around the world. Established in 1961, the library is located in the heart of Vaduz, the capital city, and serves as the central repository for books, manuscripts, periodicals, and other materials related to Liechtenstein and its history.

The library's collections are vast and diverse, encompassing a wide range of subjects and disciplines, including history, literature, art, philosophy, science, and more. Its holdings include rare books, manuscripts, maps, photographs, and archival documents, providing researchers, scholars, and students with a wealth of resources to explore and discover.

One of the library's most valuable collections is its archive of Liechtenstein-related materials, which includes historical documents, official publications, newspapers, and ephemera dating back to the principality's founding in the 18th century. These documents offer insights into Liechtenstein's political, social, and cultural evolution over the centuries, providing a valuable resource for historians, genealogists, and researchers.

In addition to its historical collections, the Liechtenstein National Library also boasts a comprehensive selection of contemporary literature and academic publications, reflecting the breadth and depth of human knowledge and creativity. From best-selling novels and scholarly journals to children's books and graphic novels, the library's shelves are stocked with a wide variety of reading material to suit every interest and age group.

The library's role extends beyond the preservation and dissemination of knowledge to include a range of educational and cultural programming. It hosts lectures, author readings, book signings, and exhibitions throughout the year, providing opportunities for the community to engage with literature, art, and ideas in a dynamic and interactive environment.

The Liechtenstein National Library also plays a vital role in supporting education and lifelong learning in Liechtenstein, offering access to research databases, online resources, and digital archives to students, teachers, and lifelong learners. Its knowledgeable staff are available to assist patrons with research inquiries, reference questions, and information requests, ensuring that everyone who walks through its doors leaves with a deeper understanding of the world around them.

Overall, the Liechtenstein National Library is much more than just a repository of books—it is a cultural institution, a community hub, and a gateway to the world of knowledge. With its rich collections, vibrant programming, and commitment to excellence, the library continues to inspire, educate, and enrich the lives of all who visit it.

The Liechtenstein Red Cross: Humanitarian Efforts in the Principality

The Liechtenstein Red Cross is a cornerstone of humanitarian efforts in the principality, dedicated to providing assistance, relief, and support to those in need both at home and abroad. Established in 1945, the organization is part of the International Red Cross and Red Crescent Movement, which operates globally to alleviate human suffering and promote respect for human dignity.

The Liechtenstein Red Cross is guided by the principles of humanity, impartiality, neutrality, independence, voluntary service, unity, and universality, which form the foundation of its mission and activities. It works in partnership with government agencies, non-governmental organizations, and other humanitarian actors to address a wide range of humanitarian challenges and emergencies, including natural disasters, conflicts, and public health crises.

One of the primary functions of the Liechtenstein Red Cross is to provide emergency response and disaster relief services during times of crisis. Its trained volunteers and staff are prepared to deploy rapidly to affected areas to assess needs, distribute aid, provide medical care, and offer psychosocial support to individuals and communities affected by disasters.

In addition to its emergency response efforts, the Liechtenstein Red Cross is actively involved in community-based programs and initiatives aimed at promoting health, safety, and well-being among the population. It offers a range of services, including first aid training, health education, social assistance, and support for vulnerable groups such as the elderly, refugees, and migrants.

The Liechtenstein Red Cross also plays a key role in promoting humanitarian values and principles through advocacy, awareness-raising, and education. It works to build public understanding and support for humanitarian action, human rights, and international humanitarian law, fostering a culture of empathy, solidarity, and compassion in Liechtenstein and beyond.

Internationally, the Liechtenstein Red Cross collaborates with sister National Red Cross and Red Crescent Societies, as well as with the International Federation of Red Cross and Red Crescent Societies (IFRC) and the International Committee of the Red Cross (ICRC), to address global humanitarian challenges and support the most vulnerable populations around the world.

Overall, the Liechtenstein Red Cross is a vital force for good in the principality, embodying the spirit of humanitarianism and serving as a beacon of hope and assistance for those in need. With its dedicated volunteers, professional staff, and commitment to humanitarian principles, the organization continues to make a positive impact on the lives of individuals and communities, both locally and globally.

Liechtenstein's Infrastructure: Communities

Transportation Connecting

Liechtenstein's transportation infrastructure plays a vital role in connecting its communities and facilitating movement within and beyond its borders. Despite its small size, the principality has developed a modern and efficient transportation network that includes roads, public transportation, and connections to neighboring countries.

Road transportation is the primary mode of travel in Liechtenstein, with a well-maintained network of highways, roads, and mountain passes that traverse the picturesque landscape of the Alps. The principality's road system is characterized by scenic routes, including the famous Vaduz-Triesenberg road, which offers breathtaking views of the Rhine Valley below.

Liechtenstein's road network is complemented by an extensive public transportation system, which includes buses and trains that serve both urban and rural areas. The Liechtenstein Bus company operates a comprehensive bus network that connects towns and villages throughout the principality, providing residents and visitors with convenient and reliable transportation options.

In addition to buses, Liechtenstein is also served by the Swiss Federal Railways (SBB), which operates train services that connect the principality to neighboring Switzerland and Austria. The train station in Schaan-Vaduz serves as the main rail hub in Liechtenstein, offering connections to major cities such as Zurich, Innsbruck, and Vienna.

Liechtenstein's strategic location in the heart of Europe makes it easily accessible by road and rail from neighboring countries. The principality is bordered by Switzerland to the west and south and Austria to the east, providing convenient access to major transportation hubs and international airports in Zurich, Geneva, and Munich.

Despite its lack of its own airport, Liechtenstein is well-connected to the global air transportation network through its proximity to international airports in neighboring countries. The Zurich Airport in Switzerland and the Altenrhein Airport in Austria are both within easy reach of Liechtenstein, offering a wide range of domestic and international flights to destinations around the world.

Overall, Liechtenstein's transportation infrastructure is a testament to its commitment to connectivity and mobility, providing residents and visitors with efficient and convenient options for traveling within the principality and beyond. Whether by road, rail, or air, Liechtenstein's transportation network ensures that its communities remain well-connected and accessible to the world.

Sustainable Development in Liechtenstein: Balancing Progress and Preservation

Sustainable development in Liechtenstein is a dynamic process that seeks to balance economic growth, social progress, and environmental protection while preserving the principality's unique heritage and natural beauty. As one of the world's smallest countries, Liechtenstein faces distinct challenges and opportunities in its pursuit of sustainability, but its commitment to innovation, collaboration, and stewardship has positioned it as a leader in sustainable development on the global stage.

One of the key pillars of Liechtenstein's approach to sustainable development is its focus on environmental conservation and resource management. The principality has implemented a range of policies and initiatives aimed at reducing carbon emissions, promoting renewable energy sources, and conserving biodiversity. Liechtenstein is also actively involved in international efforts to combat climate change, participating in agreements such as the Paris Agreement and adopting targets for greenhouse gas reduction.

In addition to environmental sustainability, Liechtenstein places a strong emphasis on social sustainability, striving to create a society that is inclusive, equitable, and resilient. The principality's social policies prioritize education, healthcare, and social welfare, ensuring that all residents have access to essential services and opportunities for personal and professional development. Liechtenstein's strong social safety net and high quality of life contribute to its reputation as one of the happiest and most prosperous countries in the world.

Economic sustainability is another key focus area for Liechtenstein, which seeks to foster a diverse and resilient economy that can thrive in a rapidly changing global landscape. The principality's economy is characterized by a strong industrial sector, innovative small and medium-sized enterprises (SMEs), and a thriving financial services industry. Liechtenstein's commitment to innovation, entrepreneurship, and investment in research and development has helped drive economic growth and create jobs while maintaining a competitive edge in international markets.

Liechtenstein's approach to sustainable development is guided by the principles of good governance, transparency, and stakeholder engagement. The principality works closely with government agencies, civil society organizations, businesses, and other stakeholders to develop and implement policies that promote sustainability and ensure that the benefits of development are shared equitably among all segments of society.

Overall, Liechtenstein's journey toward sustainable development is an ongoing endeavor that requires collaboration, innovation, and commitment from all sectors of society. By balancing progress and preservation, the principality is laying the foundation for a prosperous and sustainable future for generations to come.

Citizenship and Immigration in Liechtenstein: Rights and Responsibilities

Citizenship and immigration policies in Liechtenstein are shaped by the principality's unique history, culture, and geopolitical context. As a small, landlocked country nestled in the heart of Europe, Liechtenstein has developed its own set of rules and regulations governing who can become a citizen and who is allowed to reside within its borders.

Liechtenstein has a relatively small population, with just over 38,000 residents as of 2021. Despite its size, the principality is known for its high standard of living, low unemployment rate, and strong social welfare system, making it an attractive destination for immigrants seeking better opportunities and quality of life.

Citizenship in Liechtenstein is primarily acquired through birthright or naturalization. Individuals born to at least one Liechtenstein citizen parent automatically acquire citizenship at birth, regardless of where they are born. This principle of jus sanguinis, or right of blood, reflects Liechtenstein's emphasis on maintaining familial ties and preserving its national identity.

For those who are not born with Liechtenstein citizenship, naturalization is the primary pathway to becoming a citizen. Naturalization requirements vary depending on factors such as residency status, age, language proficiency, and integration into the local community. Generally, individuals must reside in Liechtenstein for a certain number of years, demonstrate proficiency in the German language, pass a citizenship test, and show evidence of good character and integration.

Immigration to Liechtenstein is regulated through a combination of national laws, bilateral agreements, and international treaties. Non-citizens who wish to live and work in Liechtenstein must obtain the necessary permits and visas from the government authorities. The principality offers various types of residence permits, including short-term permits for tourists and visitors, as well as long-term permits for students, workers, and family members of Liechtenstein citizens.

Liechtenstein's immigration policies are designed to balance the needs of its economy, society, and national security. The principality welcomes skilled workers, entrepreneurs, and investors who can contribute to its economic growth and innovation. At the same time, Liechtenstein is vigilant about protecting its borders and preventing illegal immigration and human trafficking.

In recent years, Liechtenstein has faced challenges related to immigration, including debates over asylum and refugee policies, integration of foreign residents, and demographic changes. The principality has implemented measures to address these challenges, such as providing language courses, cultural orientation programs, and social integration services to newcomers.

Overall, citizenship and immigration play a crucial role in shaping Liechtenstein's demographic landscape, cultural diversity, and social cohesion. By balancing rights and responsibilities, the principality seeks to create an inclusive and prosperous society that benefits both its citizens and residents alike.

Liechtenstein's Role in European Affairs: A Neutral Player's Perspective

Liechtenstein's role in European affairs is shaped by its unique position as a small, neutral country nestled between Switzerland and Austria. Despite its size, the principality actively participates in various European institutions and initiatives, contributing to regional cooperation and integration while maintaining its neutrality and independence.

Liechtenstein is not a member of the European Union (EU), but it maintains close ties with the EU through its participation in the European Free Trade Association (EFTA) and the European Economic Area (EEA) agreement. The EEA agreement allows Liechtenstein to participate in the EU's single market, facilitating trade, investment, and economic cooperation between the principality and EU member states.

As a member of the EFTA, Liechtenstein collaborates with other non-EU countries such as Norway, Iceland, and Switzerland to promote free trade and economic cooperation within Europe. The EFTA serves as a platform for dialogue and negotiation with the EU on issues such as trade policy, regulatory harmonization, and market access.

Liechtenstein also participates in other European organizations and initiatives, including the Council of Europe, the Organization for Security and Cooperation in Europe (OSCE), and various cultural and educational programs funded by the European Union. These partnerships allow Liechtenstein to engage with its European neighbors on issues of mutual interest, such as human rights, democracy, and environmental protection.

Despite its close ties with Europe, Liechtenstein maintains a policy of neutrality and non-alignment in international affairs. The principality does not belong to any military alliances and does not participate in armed conflicts or military interventions abroad. Instead, Liechtenstein focuses on diplomacy, mediation, and humanitarian aid as means of promoting peace and stability in the region and beyond.

Liechtenstein's neutrality is enshrined in its constitution and is upheld through a combination of legal, political, and diplomatic measures. The principality is committed to maintaining good relations with all countries and to serving as a bridge between different cultures, languages, and traditions in Europe.

In recent years, Liechtenstein has faced challenges related to its position in European affairs, including debates over its tax policies, financial regulations, and relationship with the EU. The principality has worked to address these challenges through dialogue, negotiation, and cooperation with its European partners, while also safeguarding its sovereignty and national interests.

Overall, Liechtenstein's role in European affairs reflects its commitment to peace, prosperity, and cooperation in the region. By actively engaging with its European neighbors while preserving its neutrality and independence, the principality contributes to the stability and well-being of Europe as a whole.

Royal Residences: Palaces and Estates of Liechtenstein's Princely Family

Royal residences hold a significant place in Liechtenstein's cultural heritage, serving as tangible symbols of the princely family's history and influence. Among the most notable of these residences is Vaduz Castle, situated on a hill overlooking the capital city of Vaduz. Dating back to the 12th century, Vaduz Castle is the official residence of the princely family and is often used for ceremonial events and official functions. While the interior of the castle is not open to the public, visitors can admire its distinctive turrets and towers from afar.

Another important royal residence in Liechtenstein is the Gutenberg Castle, located in the town of Balzers. Built in the 12th century, Gutenberg Castle is one of the oldest surviving castles in the principality and is known for its well-preserved medieval architecture. Today, the castle is privately owned and serves as a venue for cultural events, concerts, and weddings, offering visitors a glimpse into Liechtenstein's rich history and heritage.

In addition to these historic castles, the princely family also owns several estates and properties throughout Liechtenstein and beyond. One such estate is the Wilfersdorf Palace, located in Lower Austria, which has been in the possession of the princely family since the 17th century. Wilfersdorf

Palace is renowned for its elegant Baroque architecture and beautiful gardens, which attract visitors from around the world.

Liechtenstein's princely family also owns the Marschlins Castle, situated in the village of Marschlins in eastern Switzerland. This medieval castle dates back to the 13th century and has been extensively renovated and restored over the years. Today, Marschlins Castle is used as a private residence and is not open to the public, but its picturesque setting and historic charm make it a popular destination for photographers and history enthusiasts.

Beyond these notable residences, the princely family of Liechtenstein also owns a number of properties and estates in other parts of Europe, including Austria, Germany, and the Czech Republic. These properties serve as private retreats and vacation homes for the princely family, offering them a sense of privacy and seclusion away from the public eye.

Overall, the royal residences of Liechtenstein are not only architectural marvels but also important symbols of the princely family's heritage and legacy. Whether ancient castles perched on hilltops or elegant palaces surrounded by manicured gardens, these residences reflect the splendor and history of Liechtenstein's princely family for generations to come.

Liechtenstein's Philharmonic Orchestra: A Cultural Jewel in the Alps

The Liechtenstein Symphony Orchestra stands as a cultural gem in the heart of the Alps, enriching the principality's cultural landscape with its world-class performances and dedication to musical excellence. Founded in 1988, the orchestra has since become a cornerstone of Liechtenstein's cultural identity, showcasing the talent and passion of its musicians on both national and international stages.

The orchestra is composed of highly skilled musicians from Liechtenstein, Switzerland, Austria, and beyond, who come together to perform a diverse repertoire of classical, contemporary, and experimental music. Under the artistic direction of renowned conductors, the orchestra captivates audiences with its emotive interpretations and technical prowess, earning acclaim for its dynamic performances and innovative programming.

The Liechtenstein Symphony Orchestra regularly performs at prestigious venues throughout Europe, including the Vaduzer Saal in Vaduz, Liechtenstein's capital, and the Kulturhaus in Schaan. The orchestra also collaborates with leading soloists, composers, and guest conductors from around the world, further enhancing its reputation as a cultural ambassador for Liechtenstein.

In addition to its concert performances, the orchestra is committed to music education and outreach, offering workshops, masterclasses, and educational programs for aspiring musicians of all ages. Through these initiatives, the orchestra seeks to inspire a new generation of musicians and foster a deeper appreciation for music within the community.

The orchestra's commitment to excellence extends beyond the concert hall, as it actively engages in cultural diplomacy and exchange through international tours, collaborations, and residency programs. By showcasing the rich musical heritage of Liechtenstein and promoting cross-cultural dialogue, the orchestra plays a vital role in fostering connections and understanding between people from different backgrounds and traditions.

Furthermore, the Liechtenstein Symphony Orchestra is supported by the government of Liechtenstein, as well as corporate sponsors, philanthropic donors, and dedicated patrons who recognize the importance of the arts in enriching society and promoting cultural diversity. Through their support, the orchestra is able to continue its mission of bringing world-class music to audiences near and far, ensuring that Liechtenstein remains a vibrant hub of artistic creativity and expression in the heart of the Alps.

Religious Diversity in Liechtenstein: Coexistence and Harmony

Religious diversity in Liechtenstein reflects the principality's rich cultural tapestry and commitment to tolerance and coexistence. While Liechtenstein is predominantly Catholic, with Roman Catholicism being the largest religious denomination, the principality is home to a diverse array of religious communities, including Protestantism, Islam, Judaism, and others.

The Roman Catholic Church has deep historical roots in Liechtenstein and remains the dominant religious institution in the country. The majority of Liechtensteiners identify as Catholic, and the Roman Catholic Church plays a significant role in shaping the social, cultural, and moral fabric of the nation. The Prince of Liechtenstein is also traditionally a Catholic, and the Catholic Church has historically enjoyed a close relationship with the princely family.

Protestantism is the second-largest religious group in Liechtenstein, with various Protestant denominations represented, including Lutheranism and Calvinism. Protestant churches in Liechtenstein contribute to the religious diversity of the principality and provide spiritual guidance and support to their members.

In addition to Christianity, Liechtenstein is also home to small but vibrant Muslim and Jewish communities. Muslims in Liechtenstein primarily come from immigrant backgrounds, with the majority hailing from countries such as Turkey, Bosnia and Herzegovina, and Kosovo. The Muslim community in Liechtenstein is diverse, with Sunni and Shia Muslims practicing side by side and contributing to the cultural mosaic of the country.

Jews have a long history in Liechtenstein, dating back centuries, although the Jewish population today is relatively small. Despite its size, the Jewish community in Liechtenstein has made significant contributions to the cultural and intellectual life of the principality and continues to maintain a strong sense of identity and heritage.

Liechtenstein's constitution guarantees freedom of religion and belief, providing legal protections for religious minorities and ensuring that individuals have the right to practice their faith freely and openly. The government of Liechtenstein respects and values the diversity of religious traditions in the country and works to promote dialogue, understanding, and cooperation among different religious communities.

Interfaith dialogue and cooperation are promoted through various initiatives and organizations, including religious councils, interfaith forums, and community outreach programs. These efforts aim to foster mutual respect, tolerance, and harmony among people of different faiths, contributing to Liechtenstein's reputation as a peaceful and inclusive society.

Overall, religious diversity in Liechtenstein is celebrated as a source of strength and unity, reflecting the principality's commitment to pluralism, democracy, and human rights. By embracing the richness of its religious heritage and promoting interfaith cooperation, Liechtenstein continues to build a society where individuals of all backgrounds can live together in peace and harmony.

Liechtenstein's Sporting Achievements: Small Nation, Big Successes

Liechtenstein may be a small nation nestled in the heart of Europe, but when it comes to sporting achievements, it punches well above its weight. Despite its size, Liechtenstein has produced a number of world-class athletes who have made their mark on the international stage.

One of the most notable sporting achievements of Liechtenstein is its success in alpine skiing. The principality's mountainous terrain provides ideal conditions for skiing, and Liechtenstein has a strong tradition of producing talented skiers who compete in both the Winter Olympics and the World Cup circuit. Athletes like Hanni Wenzel and her brother Andreas Wenzel have achieved Olympic gold medals and World Cup victories, putting Liechtenstein on the map as a powerhouse in alpine skiing.

In addition to alpine skiing, Liechtenstein has also seen success in other winter sports, including ski jumping and cross-country skiing. Athletes like Willi Frommelt and Paul Frommelt have represented Liechtenstein with distinction in ski jumping, while athletes like Markus Hasler and Ivan Rieder have excelled in cross-country skiing, bringing home medals and accolades from international competitions.

Beyond winter sports, Liechtenstein has also made a name for itself in other athletic pursuits. Equestrian sports, for example, are popular in the principality, with riders like Julia Hassler and Marcel Bosshard competing at the highest levels of dressage and show jumping. Liechtenstein has also produced talented athletes in sports such as judo, table tennis, and athletics, who have represented the principality with pride and distinction on the global stage.

Liechtenstein's sporting achievements are not only a testament to the talent and dedication of its athletes but also to the principality's commitment to supporting sports and promoting an active lifestyle among its citizens. The government of Liechtenstein invests in sports infrastructure and facilities, including ski resorts, sports clubs, and training centers, to nurture the development of young athletes and provide them with opportunities to excel in their chosen disciplines.

Furthermore, Liechtenstein's small size fosters a strong sense of community and camaraderie among its athletes, who often receive support and encouragement from their fellow citizens. The principality's close-knit sporting community serves as a source of inspiration and motivation for aspiring athletes, driving them to achieve their goals and reach new heights of success on the international stage.

Overall, Liechtenstein's sporting achievements exemplify the spirit of determination, resilience, and excellence that defines the principality. Despite its small population and limited resources, Liechtenstein continues to produce world-class athletes who inspire and captivate audiences around the globe, earning the principality a well-deserved reputation as a powerhouse in the world of sports.

Philately and Numismatics: Liechtenstein's Contributions to the World of Collecting

Philately and numismatics, the study and collection of postage stamps and coins, respectively, have long been cherished hobbies around the world. In Liechtenstein, these pursuits hold a special significance, reflecting the principality's rich cultural heritage and its unique place in the global community of collectors.

Liechtenstein's contributions to the world of philately are significant, with the principality issuing its own postage stamps since the late 19th century. Liechtenstein's stamps are renowned for their intricate designs, high-quality printing, and thematic diversity, covering a wide range of subjects including nature, history, art, and culture. Collectors around the world eagerly seek out Liechtenstein's stamps for their rarity and aesthetic appeal, making them prized additions to any philatelic collection.

The Liechtenstein Postal Museum, located in the capital city of Vaduz, serves as a showcase for the principality's rich philatelic history. The museum houses a vast collection of postage stamps, postal artifacts, and historical documents, offering visitors insight into the evolution of Liechtenstein's postal system and the art of stamp design. The museum also hosts temporary exhibitions, educational programs, and special events, attracting philatelists and enthusiasts from near and far.

In addition to postage stamps, Liechtenstein is also known for its contributions to the field of numismatics, or the study of coins and currency. The principality has a long numismatic tradition, with coins minted in Liechtenstein bearing unique designs and symbols that reflect the country's cultural heritage and history. Liechtenstein's commemorative coins, in particular, are highly sought after by collectors for their artistic merit and historical significance.

The Liechtenstein National Museum houses a comprehensive collection of coins and currency, spanning various periods of the principality's history. From ancient Roman coins to modern-day euro coins, the museum's exhibits offer a fascinating glimpse into Liechtenstein's monetary history and the evolution of numismatic art. Visitors to the museum can explore rare and valuable coins from around the world, as well as learn about the process of coin production and the role of currency in shaping societies.

Beyond museums and collections, Liechtenstein also hosts philatelic and numismatic events, including stamp and coin fairs, auctions, and exhibitions. These events provide opportunities for collectors to buy, sell, and trade stamps and coins, as well as connect with fellow enthusiasts and experts in the field. The principality's vibrant philatelic and numismatic community continues to thrive, fueled by a passion for collecting and a dedication to preserving Liechtenstein's cultural heritage for future generations.

Overall, Liechtenstein's contributions to the world of philately and numismatics are a testament to the principality's rich history, artistic talent, and commitment to cultural preservation. Whether through postage stamps or coins, Liechtenstein's unique creations continue to captivate collectors and enthusiasts worldwide, leaving an indelible mark on the global community of collectors for generations to come.

Liechtenstein's Health Care System: Prioritizing Well-being for All

Liechtenstein's health care system is built on the principles of accessibility, quality, and affordability, ensuring that residents have access to comprehensive medical services and treatments. As a small principality with a population of around 38,000 people, Liechtenstein's health care system is characterized by its efficiency and personalized approach to care.

The health care system in Liechtenstein is primarily funded through a combination of public and private sources. The government of Liechtenstein allocates funds to support public health initiatives, hospitals, and clinics, while private health insurance supplements coverage for additional services and treatments. This dual system ensures that residents have access to a wide range of medical services, from preventive care to specialized treatments, without facing financial barriers.

Liechtenstein's health care system is governed by the Health Insurance Act, which mandates that all residents must have health insurance coverage. The majority of residents are covered under the country's compulsory health insurance scheme, which provides access to basic medical services and treatments. Private health insurance plans offer additional coverage for services such as dental care, vision care, and alternative therapies, allowing residents to tailor their coverage to their individual needs.

Primary care in Liechtenstein is provided by a network of general practitioners and family doctors, who serve as the first point of contact for patients seeking medical care. These primary care physicians play a crucial role in promoting preventive health measures, diagnosing and treating common ailments, and coordinating care for patients with chronic conditions.

For more specialized medical services, residents may be referred to one of Liechtenstein's hospitals or clinics. The principality is home to several hospitals and medical centers, equipped with modern facilities and staffed by skilled medical professionals. In cases where specialized care is not available locally, patients may be referred to hospitals in neighboring Switzerland or Austria, with whom Liechtenstein has reciprocal health care agreements.

Liechtenstein places a strong emphasis on preventive health care, with initiatives aimed at promoting healthy lifestyles and reducing the incidence of chronic diseases. The government supports programs and campaigns focused on nutrition, physical activity, smoking cessation, and mental health awareness, aiming to improve overall well-being and quality of life for residents.

In addition to traditional medical care, Liechtenstein also recognizes the importance of complementary and alternative therapies in promoting holistic health. Alternative therapies such as acupuncture, homeopathy, and naturopathy are widely practiced and accepted in Liechtenstein, with many residents incorporating these treatments into their health care routines alongside conventional medicine.

Overall, Liechtenstein's health care system is designed to prioritize the well-being of all residents, ensuring that they have access to high-quality medical care and services when needed. By combining public and private resources, promoting preventive health measures, and embracing a holistic approach to care, Liechtenstein continues to uphold its commitment to providing comprehensive health care for all.

Family Life in Liechtenstein: Traditions and Values Passed Down Generations

Family life in Liechtenstein is deeply rooted in tradition and values that have been passed down through generations. As a small principality nestled in the Alps, Liechtenstein has a close-knit community where family plays a central role in daily life.

One of the defining features of family life in Liechtenstein is its emphasis on strong familial bonds and support networks. Families in Liechtenstein tend to be close-knit, with multiple generations often living in close proximity to one another. This close family structure fosters a sense of unity and belonging, with family members providing emotional, financial, and practical support to one another in times of need.

Traditionally, family life in Liechtenstein has been characterized by a division of labor based on gender roles. While men have historically been responsible for providing for the family financially, women have typically taken on the role of managing the household and caring for children. However, in recent years, there has been a shift towards more egalitarian family dynamics, with both men and women sharing responsibilities both at home and in the workplace.

Education is highly valued in Liechtenstein, and families place a strong emphasis on providing their children with the best possible educational opportunities. The principality boasts a high-quality education system, with public schools offering free education up to the secondary level. Additionally, Liechtenstein is home to several prestigious international schools, providing families with options for a diverse and enriching educational experience for their children.

Religion also plays a significant role in family life in Liechtenstein, with the majority of the population identifying as Roman Catholic. Religious traditions and values are passed down through generations, with families participating in religious ceremonies, holidays, and rituals together. The Catholic Church plays an active role in the community, providing support and guidance to families in matters of faith and morality.

In addition to traditional family structures, Liechtenstein also recognizes and supports diverse family arrangements, including single-parent families, blended families, and same-sex families. The principality has enacted legislation to protect the rights of all families, ensuring that they have access to legal recognition, support services, and social benefits.

Overall, family life in Liechtenstein is characterized by strong bonds, shared values, and a commitment to nurturing the well-being and happiness of all family members. Whether through traditional customs or evolving social norms, families in Liechtenstein continue to uphold the rich traditions and values that have been passed down through generations, ensuring that family remains at the heart of community life in the principality.

Environmental Conservation in Liechtenstein: Preserving the Alpine Ecosystem

Environmental conservation in Liechtenstein is a vital aspect of the principality's commitment to preserving its natural beauty and biodiversity. Nestled in the heart of the Alps, Liechtenstein boasts stunning landscapes, rich biodiversity, and pristine ecosystems that are cherished by residents and visitors alike.

One of the primary focuses of environmental conservation in Liechtenstein is the protection of its alpine ecosystem. The principality is home to a diverse range of flora and fauna, including rare and endangered species such as the ibex, chamois, and golden eagle. Efforts to safeguard these species and their habitats are paramount to ensuring the long-term health and sustainability of Liechtenstein's natural environment.

Liechtenstein has implemented various policies and initiatives to promote environmental conservation and sustainable development. The government works closely with environmental organizations, research institutions, and local communities to address key environmental challenges such as habitat loss, pollution, and climate change. These efforts include the establishment of protected areas, the implementation of conservation projects, and the promotion of sustainable land management practices.

One notable example of environmental conservation in Liechtenstein is the creation of nature reserves and protected areas. The principality is home to several designated nature reserves, national parks, and protected landscapes that serve as important refuges for native wildlife and plant species. These protected areas not only safeguard biodiversity but also provide opportunities for outdoor recreation, nature-based tourism, and scientific research.

Liechtenstein also places a strong emphasis on sustainable energy and resource management. The principality has invested in renewable energy sources such as hydroelectric power, solar energy, and biomass, reducing its reliance on fossil fuels and mitigating greenhouse gas emissions. Additionally, efforts to promote energy efficiency, waste reduction, and recycling contribute to the overall sustainability of Liechtenstein's economy and society.

Education and public awareness play a crucial role in environmental conservation efforts in Liechtenstein. The government, along with environmental organizations and educational institutions, conducts outreach programs, environmental campaigns, and environmental education initiatives to raise awareness about environmental issues and promote sustainable behaviors among residents and visitors.

Community involvement is also key to the success of environmental conservation in Liechtenstein. Local residents, businesses, and community groups actively participate in conservation projects, volunteer initiatives, and environmental stewardship programs, demonstrating a shared commitment to protecting the principality's natural heritage for future generations.

In conclusion, environmental conservation in Liechtenstein is a multifaceted endeavor that encompasses policy, education, community engagement, and scientific research. By prioritizing the preservation of its alpine ecosystem and adopting sustainable practices, Liechtenstein is paving the way for a greener, more resilient future, where nature and people can thrive in harmony.

Future Prospects: Challenges and Opportunities for Liechtenstein

As Liechtenstein looks toward the future, it faces a unique set of challenges and opportunities that will shape its trajectory in the years to come. One of the foremost challenges is balancing economic growth with environmental sustainability. As a small, landlocked nation, Liechtenstein must carefully manage its natural resources and limit its ecological footprint while fostering innovation and economic development.

Another challenge lies in maintaining its position as a global financial center while adhering to international regulations and standards. Liechtenstein's banking sector plays a significant role in its economy, but increasing scrutiny and regulation from international bodies require the principality to adapt and evolve its financial services industry to remain competitive.

Demographic shifts and an aging population present additional challenges for Liechtenstein. Like many countries in Europe, Liechtenstein faces the dual challenges of an aging population and declining birth rates. Addressing these demographic trends will require innovative solutions to ensure a skilled workforce, support social welfare programs, and maintain economic vitality.

Technological advancements present both challenges and opportunities for Liechtenstein's future. While innovation drives economic growth and fosters new industries, it also raises questions about data privacy, cybersecurity, and the ethical implications of emerging technologies. Liechtenstein must navigate these complexities to harness the benefits of technological progress while mitigating potential risks.

Globalization and geopolitical shifts also pose challenges for Liechtenstein's future. As a small nation in the heart of Europe, Liechtenstein must navigate an increasingly interconnected world while safeguarding its sovereignty and cultural identity. The principality's commitment to neutrality and international cooperation will be essential in navigating geopolitical challenges and fostering peaceful relations with its neighbors.

Despite these challenges, Liechtenstein also possesses significant opportunities for growth and prosperity. Its strategic location, stable political environment, and highly skilled workforce position it as an attractive destination for investment and business development. The principality's commitment to innovation, entrepreneurship, and sustainable development further enhances its appeal as a dynamic and forward-thinking nation.

Liechtenstein's small size and agile government enable it to adapt quickly to changing circumstances and seize opportunities for growth and diversification. By leveraging its strengths, fostering collaboration across sectors, and embracing innovation, Liechtenstein can overcome its challenges and chart a path toward a prosperous and sustainable future for generations to come.

Epilogue

In this epilogue, we reflect on the journey we've taken through the vibrant and dynamic landscape of Liechtenstein. From its rich history to its breathtaking natural beauty, this small principality nestled in the heart of Europe has captured our imagination and left an indelible mark on our hearts.

As we conclude our exploration of Liechtenstein, it's clear that this tiny nation punches above its weight in many respects. Its fascinating history, from the rise of the Liechtenstein dynasty to its emergence as a modern constitutional monarchy, offers a glimpse into the resilience and adaptability of its people.

Liechtenstein's unique political landscape, characterized by its status as a constitutional monarchy and its commitment to direct democracy, reflects its dedication to democratic principles and civic engagement. The principality's governance model, which blends tradition with innovation, serves as a testament to its ability to evolve and thrive in a rapidly changing world.

The geography of Liechtenstein, with its rugged alpine terrain and pristine natural landscapes, provides the backdrop for a wide range of outdoor activities and adventures. Whether hiking through the mountains, skiing down the slopes of Malbun, or exploring the tranquil valleys and meadows, Liechtenstein offers endless opportunities to connect with nature and experience the beauty of the Alps.

The cultural richness of Liechtenstein is evident in its diverse array of festivals, arts, and traditions. From the vibrant celebrations of Fasnacht to the world-class exhibitions at the Kunstmuseum Liechtenstein, the principality's cultural scene is alive with creativity and expression.

Liechtenstein's culinary delights, blending alpine flavors with international influences, tantalize the taste buds and offer a delicious window into its gastronomic heritage. Whether savoring a hearty cheese fondue, indulging in a traditional käsknöpfle, or enjoying a glass of locally produced wine, Liechtenstein's cuisine is sure to delight even the most discerning palate.

As we bid farewell to Liechtenstein, we carry with us memories of its stunning landscapes, rich history, and warm hospitality. Our journey through this enchanting principality has been a testament to the resilience, creativity, and spirit of its people. As Liechtenstein looks towards the future, we can only imagine the exciting adventures and discoveries that lie ahead for this small but mighty nation in the heart of Europe.

Printed in Great Britain
by Amazon